MW01228438

All-Time Sports Records

BASKETBALL RECORDS

MARK WEAKLAND

BLACK
RABBIT
BOOKS

Bolt is published by Black Rabbit Books
P.O. Box 3263, Mankato, Minnesota, 56002.
www.blackrabbitbooks.com
Copyright © 2021 Black Rabbit Books

Jen Besel, editor; Catherine Cates, designer;
Omay Ayres, photo researcher

All rights reserved. No part of this book may be reproduced,
stored in a retrieval system or transmitted in any form or by any means,
electronic, mechanical, photocopying, recording, or otherwise, without written
permission from the publisher.

Library of Congress Cataloging-in-Publication Data
Names: Weakland, Mark, author.
Title: Basketball records / by Mark Weakland.
Other titles: Bolt (North Mankato, Minn.)
Description: Mankato, Minnesota : Bolt | Black Rabbit Books, 2021. |
Series: Bolt. All-time sports records | Includes webography. | Audience:
Ages: 4-12 years. | Audience: Grades: 4-6.
Identifiers: LCCN 2019027599 (print) | ISBN 9781623102395 (Hardcover) |
ISBN 9781644663356 (Paperback) | ISBN 9781623103330 (eBook)
Subjects: LCSH: Basketball—Records—United States—Juvenile literature. |
Basketball—Records—Canada—Juvenile literature. | Basketball players—Rating of—
Juvenile literature. | National Basketball Association—History—Juvenile literature.
Classification: LCC GV885.55 .W43 2021 (print) | LCC GV885.55 (ebook) |
DDC 796.323—dc23
LC record available at https://lccn.loc.gov/2019027599
LC ebook record available at https://lccn.loc.gov/2019027600

Printed in the United States. 2/20

All records and statistics are current as of 2019.

Image Credits

Alamy: Cal Sport Media, 16–17;
Chris Poss, 8–9; Rich Kane Photogra-
phy, Cover; AP Images: Al Messerschmidt
Archive, 14; GENE HERRICK, 24; KIRTHMON
DOZIER, 29; Lennox McLendon, 10; RAY STUB-
BLEBINE, 6–7; Richard Hartog, 1; Dreamstime: Jerry
Coli, 4–5; en.wikipedia.org: Vjmlhds, , 26; Newscom:
Darrell Walker/Icon SMI 945, 20; HARRY E. WALKER/
MCT, 23; Jim Ruymen UPI, 18; Mingo Nesmith/Icon
Sportswire DIL, 9; Shutterstock: Cherdchai charasri,
20–21, 32; Christos Georghiou, 12–13, 26–27;
EFKS, 12–13; kapona, 31; mipan, 6; Pierre E.
Debbas, 3; Sudowoodo, 26–27
Every effort has been made to contact
copyright holders for material reproduced
in this book. Any omissions will be
rectified in subsequent printings
if notice is given to
the publisher.

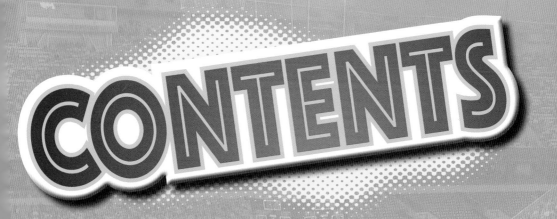

CONTENTS

CHAPTER 1

Powerful PLAYERS

Towering players rush down the court. Their steps sound like thunder. One dribbles then tosses the ball. Another catches it as he leaps. Wham! He slams the ball into the hoop.

Basketball is an exciting sport. New records are set each season. But some records are so amazing, they might never be broken.

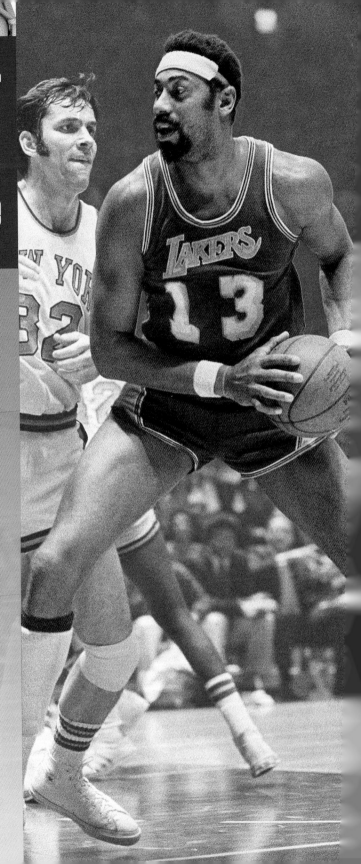

Times a Player Scored 60 or More Points in One Game

32 TIMES
Wilt Chamberlain

6 TIMES
Kobe Bryant

5 TIMES
Michael Jordan

4 TIMES
Elgin Baylor

CHAPTER 2

Unbelievable RECORDS

RECORD!

Most Points Scored in One NBA Season **4,029**

Wilt Chamberlain could score like no one else. He set many records. Some may never be broken. He is the only player to score 4,000 points in one season. He is also the only player to score 100 points in one game.

Diana Taurasi has great **focus**. She is a fierce player. And she holds the WNBA record for the most 3-point shots. She's made 1,102 so far. She also holds the WNBA record for most **career** points at 8,575. And she's likely to make more.

• • • • • • • • • • • • • • • • • •

In one 2018 game, Liz Cambage was on fire. She pulled down 10 **rebounds**. She blocked five shots. And she scored 53 points. Her score was a new WNBA record.

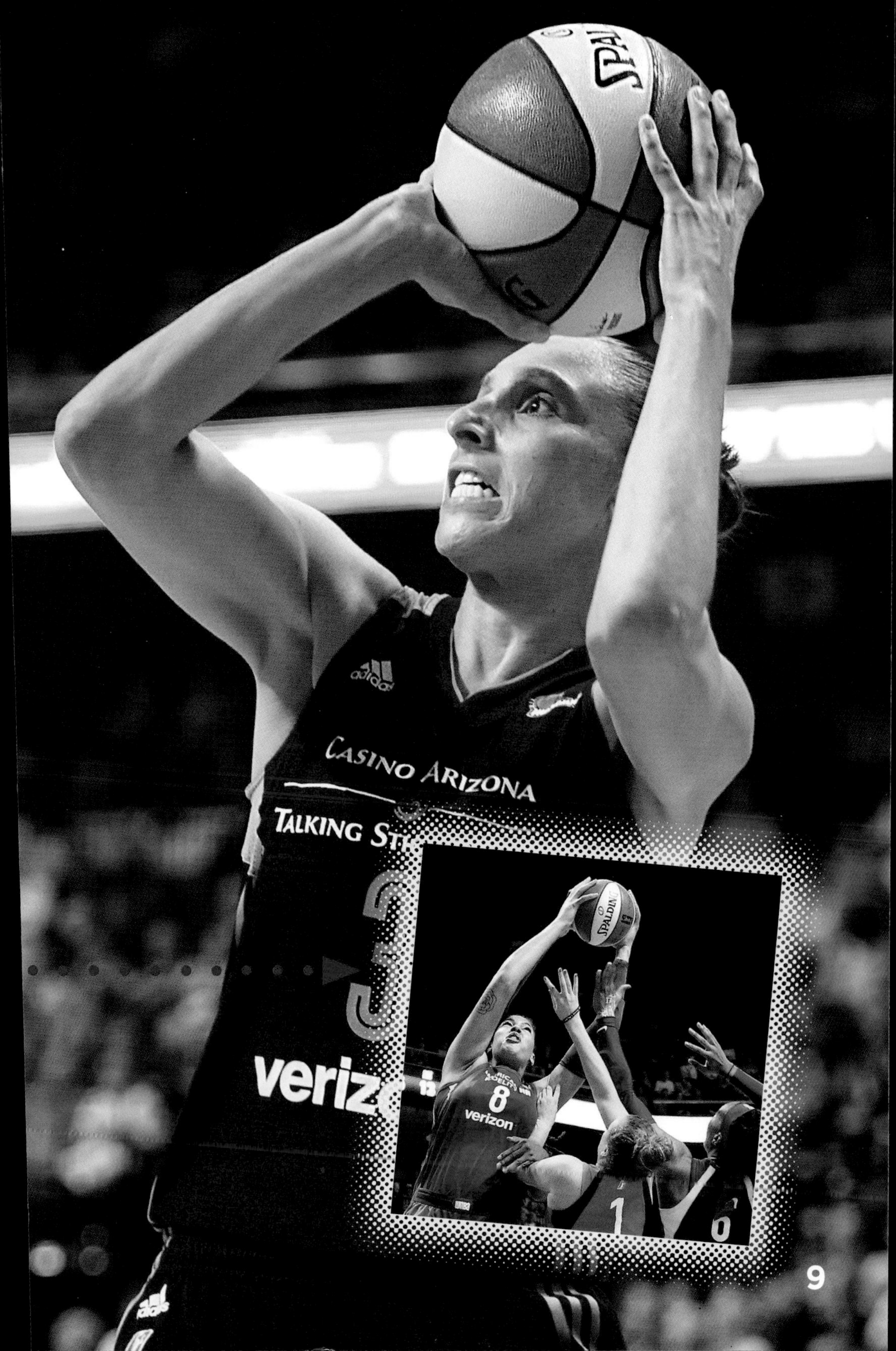
CASINO ARIZONA
SPALDING
8
verizon

• • • • • • Kareem Abdul-Jabbar played 20 years in the NBA. At more than 7 feet (2 meters) tall, he was a giant. But that's not why he was great. He was a smart player with many skills. In his career, he scored 38,387 points. It is a record that may never be matched.

8,600

8,400 — 8,575

8,200

8,000

7,800

7,600

7,400 — 7,488

7,200 — 7,380

7,000

total career points

DIANA
TAURASI

TINA
THOMPSON

TAMIKA
CATCHINGS

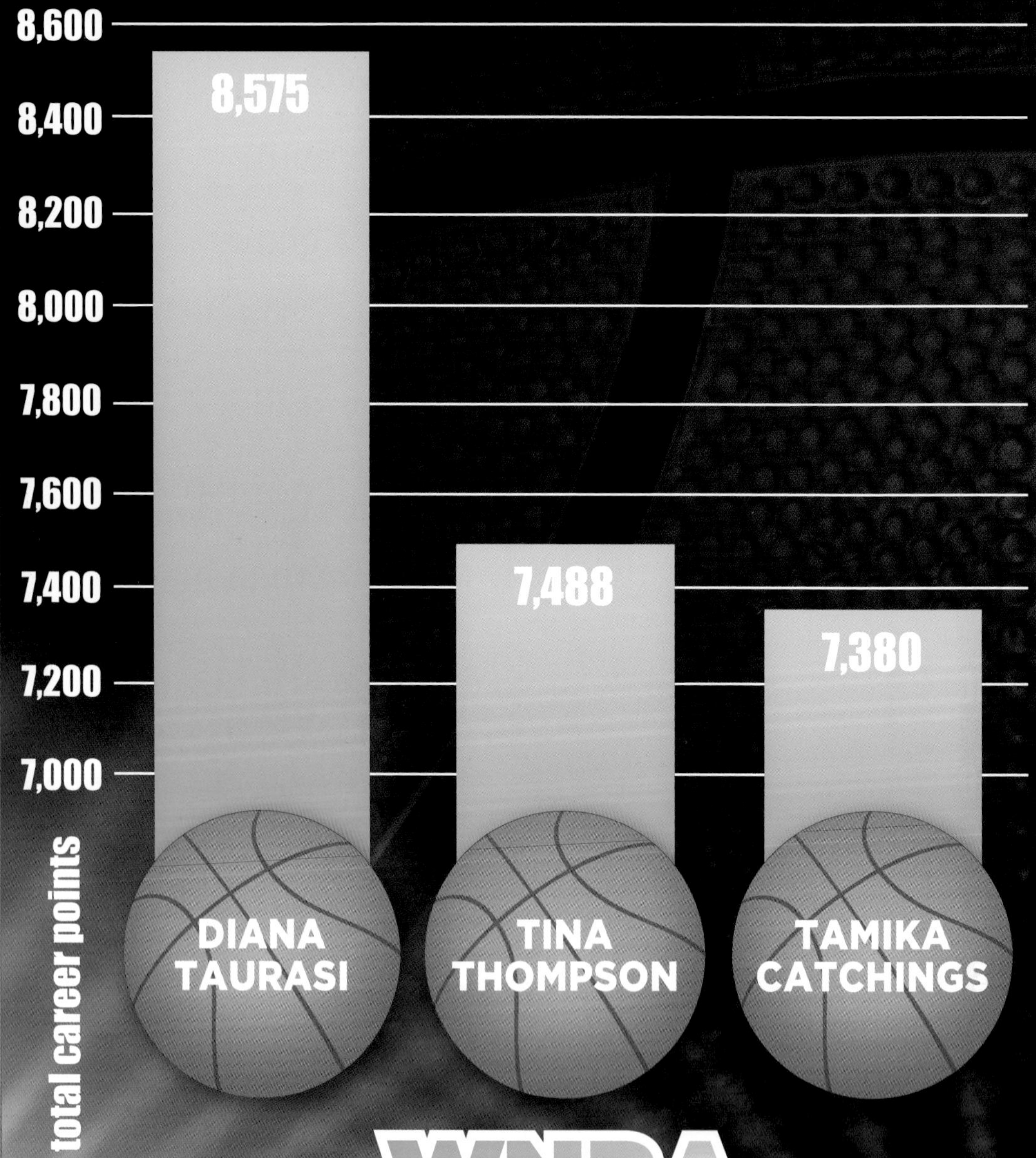

WNBA

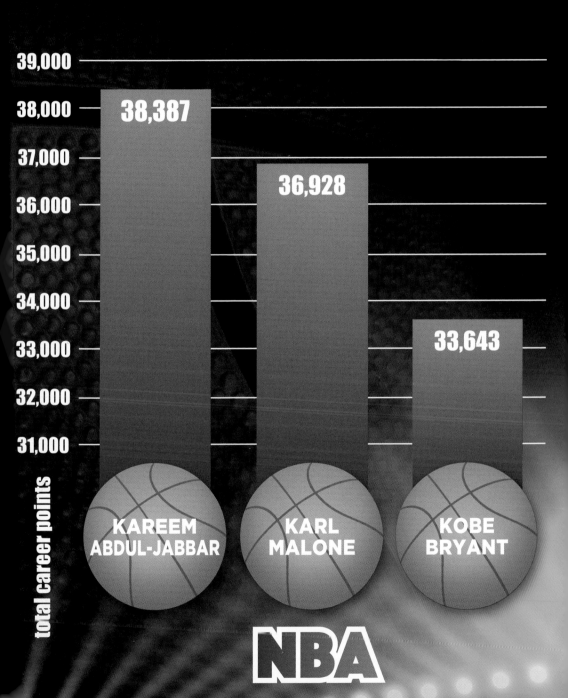

total career points

39,000
38,000 — 38,387
37,000
36,000 — 36,928
35,000
34,000
33,000 — 33,643
32,000
31,000

KAREEM
ABDUL-JABBAR

KARL
MALONE

KOBE
BRYANT

NBA

Jordan scored 15 or more points in every **playoff** game he played.

Michael Jordan was one of the NBA's most exciting players. He could leap from 15 feet (5 m) out and slam the ball through the hoop. He led his team to six NBA championships. In a 1986 playoff game, he scored a record 63 points.

Tamika Catchings played in the • • • • • •
WNBA for 15 years. She was fast.
She was fearless. Her skills helped
her set a record for most **steals**.
In her career, she stole the ball
1,074 times.

In 15 years, Catchings made 3,316 rebounds.
nly two other WNBA players have more career rebounds.

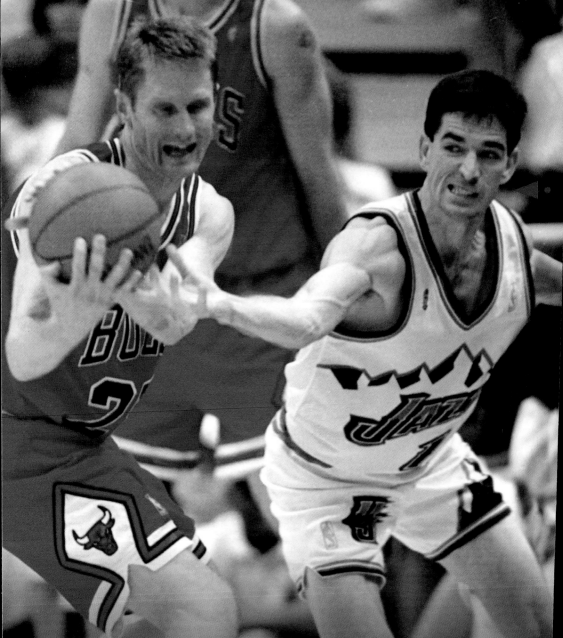

Most NBA Career Steals

John Stockton	Jason Kidd	Michael Jordan	Gary Payton	Maurice Chee
3,265	2,684	2,514	2,445	2,31(

• • • • •John Stockton played great defense. He leaped, darted, and twisted to steal the ball from his **opponents**. Stockton holds the NBA record for steals. He pulled off 3,265 of them. He also had 15,806 career **assists**. He holds the record for that too.

FINALS MVP AWARDS

DIANA TAURASI
(Phoenix Mercury)

LISA LESLIE
(Los Angeles Sparks)

SYLVIA FOWLES
(Minnesota Lynx)

CYNTHIA COOPER
(Houston Comets)

CHAMPIONSHIP TITLES

PLAYERS WITH THE MOST NBA

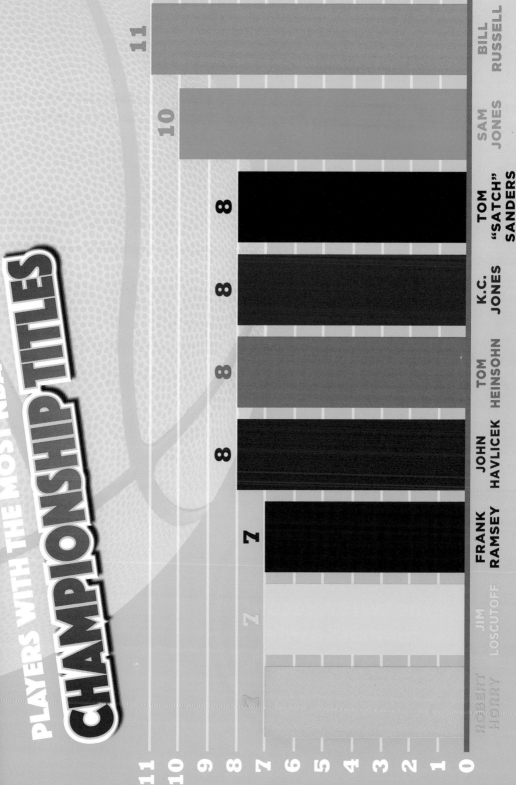

Player	Titles
BILL RUSSELL	11
SAM JONES	10
TOM "SATCH" SANDERS	8
K.C. JONES	8
TOM HEINSOHN	8
JOHN HAVLICEK	8
FRANK RAMSEY	7
JIM LOSCUTOFF	7
ROBERT HORRY	7

RECORD!
Most Games Started in the WNBA 508

Sue Bird is a superstar point guard. She had to miss the 2019 season due to injury. But she still holds the WNBA record for most games started. In 16 seasons, she started 508 games.

Bird also holds the WNBA record for most career assists with 2,831.

23

Most NBA Championships Won in a Row

Boston Celtics 1959–1966	Chicago Bulls 1991–1993
8 TITLES	**3** TITLES

It's rare for a team to win even three championships in a row. But the Boston Celtics won eight NBA titles without a break. How did it do it? The team had talented players. And it had a great coach. For eight special years, the Celtics team was the best in the world.

Chicago Bulls	Los Angeles Lakers	Minneapolis Lakers
1996–1998	2000–2002	1952–1954
3	**3**	**3**
TITLES	TITLES	TITLES

MOST NBA AND WNBA CHAMPIONSHIPS WON

CHICAGO BULLS	6
GOLDEN STATE/ PHILADELPHIA WARRIORS	6
LOS ANGELES/ MINNEAPOLIS LAKERS	
BOSTON CELTICS	

0   2   4   6

WNBA

DETROIT SHOCK
3

LOS ANGELES SPARKS
3

PHOENIX MERCURY
3

NBA

16

17

8   10   12   14   16   18

SEATTLE STORM

3

HOUSTON COMETS

4

MINNESOTA LYNX

4

CHAPTER 3

More to SCORE

Basketball players leap and shoot. They jump and block. Lunging, they steal a ball and race down the court. Few people can do what they do. These players are gifted athletes. And their records thrill and excite fans everywhere.

assist (uh-SIST)—the action, such as a pass, of a player who helps a teammate to score

career (kuh-REER)—a period of time spent in a job

focus (FO-kus)—directed attention

opponent (uh-POH-nunt)—a person, team, or group that is competing against another

playoff (PLAY-ahf)—a series of games played after the regular season to decide which player or team is the champion

rebound (RE-bownd)—to take possession of the ball after it bounces off the backboard or rim

steal (STEEL)—to take from another player

BOOKS

Adamson, Thomas K. *Basketball Records.* Incredible Sports Records. Minneapolis: Bellwether Media, Inc., 2018.

Hellebuyck, Adam, and Laura Deimel. *NBA Finals.* Global Citizens: Sports. Ann Arbor, MI: Cherry Lake Publishing, 2019.

Segal, Adam Elliott. *Basketball Stars.* Richmond Hill, Ontario: Firefly Books, 2017.

WEBSITES

Basketball
www.ducksters.com/sports/basketball.php

Fun Facts for Kids about Basketball
easyscienceforkids.com/basketball-hang-time-video-for-kids/

Jr. NBA
jr.nba.com/

INDEX